D1602113

FEELINGS of AND

BARRY SCHWABSKY

BSE

ISBN: 978-1-7363248-6-8

BSE Books are distributed by
  Small Press Distribution
  1341 Seventh Street
  Berkeley, CA 94710
  orders@spdbooks.org | www.spdbooks.org
  1-800-869-7553

BSE Books can also be purchased at
www.blacksquareeditions.org and www.hyperallergic.com

Contributions to BSE can be made to
  Off the Park Press, Inc.
  976 Kensington Ave.
  Plainfield, NJ 07060
  (Please make checks payable to Off the Park Press, Inc.)

To contact the Press please write:
  Black Square Editions
  1200 Broadway, Suite 3C
  New York, NY 10001

An independent subsidiary of Off the Park Press, Inc.

Member of CLMP.

Publisher: John Yau
Editors: Ronna Lebo and Boni Joi
Design & composition: Shanna Compton

Cover art: Matthew Wong, "A Poet's World" (2015), ink on rice paper, 62¾ x 31½ inches. © 2021 Matthew Wong Foundation / Artists Rights Society (ARS).

We ought to say a feeling of *and*, a feeling of *if*,
a feeling of *but*, and a feeling of *by*, quite as readily
as we say a feeling of *blue* or a feeling of *cold*.

—William James, *Principles of Psychology*

Contents

I

The Selected Cosmos

Tangled breath. They said
it wasn't finished yet. I also
heard myself say that
and didn't know what
to think. Good feelings yesterday
don't help me today. In the meantime
I'm an ordinary mortal
and have never known
more pleasant trial. Magic: not
what I'd call a downfall
though (yes) a threat
to house and home. More the birth
of surprise, a swamp
of divergent views because, after all,
can the mind ever be fully
occupied? Thoughts are instant
and without rash consequence
—preferably. We went in search
of places words go
to make out. Of frenzied sun.
Unholy racket. The sky
makes even less sense now
but as a map of ways to lose
your way this fresh
evening air may force the door
of departure. How open

your mouth could be. Two mugs
exchange halos on a late bus
downtown. In truth, dissenting
orations make for fine
funerals. That's all the air
in my nostrils for now. Hardly two
breaths to my name but living
cautiously like grass that bends
before each wind. Mouths
of religion, minds of disbelief.

We wanted more lovable
gods, a blind sky tossed
over distracted misdemeanors.
Or Godzilla, a way of making
radiation visible. But who will tell him
this is poetry? It's always
sort of, isn't it? Listen
to its resistance. The door
shuts the house. Swans glide
like shadows of death. The park fills
with Sunday people. Quiet
your throat. This,
the candid hour.

Afterthought

These gardens of the ruined world
sadly used yet still very good
in a twilight of threadbare insignia

You couldn't make it up
but in the time it takes to pick at a scab
peering into your pupil she fell asleep

Unbuckling the halo from your image
the stars pawing at my eyes
vanity of vanities

A woman is still a woman
but sometimes not
the other way round.

Christmas on Earth, Noon on the Moon

Grainy secrets for a newer sea
that star took place so far away
we watched it myopic from the belvedere

a solitary eye cuts light into words
from which some intimate plasma spreads
pale yellow in sudden cracks, paying no mind

yes to all changes to past tense
its stories sensibly filed under dramaturgy
sometimes hard to make out what color they are

sticky vowels dribble into them
from a clockwork heliostat, an antique
they loiter damaged around the loved one's thighs

nibbling at some sugar maple gloom
sweet knowledge saved up or drowned
in the stifled promise of an airless year.

An Inclusive Disjunction

Eyes decisively screwed into place
yet nostrils breathe denial
next stop: indignant sparrow's bad luck

I still haven't seen you
a bitter tone leaches through the tree line
it holds you up to daylight
under layers of survival gear

we never thought we'd know what we wanted
or start to see with the bright eyes of a cat
we're still trying to pick up your faint signal
the thin light of a broken star.

Wretches of the Earth

Our angular days are over
no more tormenting me with intervals
inside a poem in the style of
each one you know

you hear the telephone keep ringing
as you ward off its blows
it rains and it rains and it rains
and it rains for a fixed term

of our wretched animal existence
a fold-out atlas
that's seen better days
than I've been feeling for a while

and still recurs in my nightmares
of this dingy coffee bar
where time is a page on a calendar
that no one ever tears off

photography is not to blame
for changing daylight into silver
our angular days are over
and the thirsty pastel nights begin.

A Breathing Giant

First you found me pinned up
against a wrapping paper sky
that was the start

you took a picture
I might have seemed exposed
but still your "no" was stripped so bare

undiscovered by clouds
I stay loyal to the fog
from which I watch you unwind me

—when first you found me pinned up
against a wrapping paper sky
that was the start.

What We Do, What We Don't

Two people talking
talk about something
but the way they talk

as if it were nothing
a yes dropped in passing
a blister pearl of song

or the rustling of a summer dress
or of the breeze that sets it aquiver
that's flattery

yes you can dance to it
a late word casts no shadow
a dark sound sheds no light

most sounds want to rise
to kiss the skylight
and disappear

but in march the wooden soldiers
their rumbling footsteps
slow them down.

Something to Forget Me By

Please silence
your cells phones now.

Darkness undresses
in darkness, in surcease,

prepares nightmares where
most expected. I call you

my twilight idol, my southern
dust. How colors vibrate is their

damn business. Now I ascribe your
face to some clouds

at sunset: one eye open,
the other closed. The one,

glaring, accused but saw
nothing. The other, sealed,

disconsolate, understands
these leftover thoughts:

receptive syrup, a specious eye,
the sea yet another idolatry

and your sighing song rehearsed
for my weary funeral.

Reverse Cowgirl's Lullaby

The human flesh search engine
for the love that shadows know
this was just after my burnout fellowship
the past smelt of stale bread and cleaning fluid

she asked a poem to float in through the window
to look without humming its meaning
she said my silence
has the color of a headache

and saw
a foolish star
drinking moon milk
it failed to exercise portion control

personally I don't see the issue
nothing much happens most times
until—wham!—it does
and you surrender to sleep, sleep.

With Love from Your Favorite Metaphor

Enter fog / new word down a notch / ice cream
in the sun / getting warm and drippy
in the eye of love / you feel as you turn
and twist / it's all about the voice / god's
shadow / the size of a pencil eraser / obsessively
packaging, aren't you? / we recognize
the stupidity of our thoughts / best three
out of five / good curtains make good neighbors / rewriting
what they put in my hand / glowing with the radiance
of / not even sure myself what it is I am
asking / liquid teeth / do we identify or disidentify
and in what way / yes, the whole
wad / like smoke in my nostril / when we took
romanticism indoors / you said, won't you
ask me to stop / who wore contagious eyes / saw through
the meaning of stop / hurriedly nettled / commence
increase / agreement absorbing salts / you said, won't you
ask me to stop / groan upbraided / you said stop
halfway to window / ask me to crowd a room
with a stare / when we took your romanticism
indoors / gothic tech house / passing into silence not
going anywhere / the floating tone falls
after flying colors rise or rinse / to draw out
the ghost who used to be me.

II

René Ricard Dream

In the dream I had last night
I was crossing the road in London
(I think it was Mile End Road)
when I literally bumped into René Ricard.

He was carrying a load of notebooks
and other personal items. He pushed them
into my hands, saying, I think
you could use these. I walked on

carrying them and stepped into a pub
where I could sit down and read them.
I was well aware that what had just
happened was extraordinary since

I knew in the dream that he had died.
I was amazed that I had been chosen
to receive these things since although
I had met René I did not "know" him.

Apparently the pub that I'd found
was one where he was a regular
because the people there recognized
that the stuff I had was his and they

asked about that. They didn't show suspicion
but wonderment. The next thing I knew
I was at my friend Scott's house
in Islington, still with René's stuff,

telling Scott what had happened
but he didn't know who René was
and I had to explain it to him. On
waking, I began to wonder

whether René had ever actually lived
in London. Somehow I doubt it.

Postscript to René Ricard Dream

Sage Robert advises that my dream
could mislead—"if it implies that René
was a great poet, which he was not,
imo. He had rare talents

but they lay elsewhere." To live
in strangers' dreams is talent indeed.
But is the René Ricard of my dream
René Ricard in person? Nothing

in dreams is entirely what we imagine.
This René Ricard of London looked
nothing like the one who walked
Manhattan's streets. He more resembled

Gary Indiana. The High Priestess
of the Temple of Oshun says
mind my homework. But my René or Gary
gives permission to slough it off on you.

Polonaise Fantaisie

Strange gestures of musicians. The way a pianist might draw a hand up with resolve, as if to entice some weighty chord to linger in the air just that much longer, or even haul a stray note bodily from the abyss of the keyboard as one would a child that has tumbled into the well. What bothers me is how this useless coaxing sometimes seems to work.

Another Pianist

He tears certain notes right off the keyboard
leaving ragged edges
and two or three tiny spots of blood.

Moderato (Pour la main gauche)

In this prelude the left hand expresses
its lonely ache for the right and lets
abandoned notes stray at large
through the starry chill of the night.

Cartesian Medication

No mind
no body
no problem.

In Memory of John Cage

Silence was his golden oldie.

Conversation with a Revolutionary

I had to agree that politics is a higher calling than art. But not, I insisted, a more productive one, since the chances of turning out to have made a good revolution are even less than those of having made a good painting.

The Bourgeois Poet

Her parents had eccentric expectations. While their friends destined their offspring for the law, finance, good marriages, they hoped for a poet in the family. But she rebelled and became, despite everything, a poet.

Bouquet

If the flowers are you
in this enormous hospital
who gets to be the invalid?

A Partial List of Omissions
for Mel Chin

I

Here between Spain and Technetium we should find, for instance, the genus Spalax, those blind mole rats whose eyes are completely covered by a layer of skin; their eyes are eyes in God's memory alone. Here too one should learn about undesirable electronic messages and pork-based mystery meats of whose name I have no need to remind you. In Spaoh, in the state of Sarwak, I would have you know, a salted pufferfish known as Ikan Masin Buntal is the local delicacy. And wouldn't it be nice to be shown how to prepare spätzle, whether savory or sweet? Speed of light, speed of sound, speed metal—where are they when we need them? Spin doctors, spin-offs, and spinning jennies belong here too, along with the stab-in-the-back-myth or Dolchstoßlegende according to which the German army would have won the Great War had it not been betrayed by the country's craven civilians, and statology, that pagan worship of the state proclaimed by Giovanni Gentile in the name of Mussolini and decried by Pope Pius XI—all these layered together between a book's covers like a submarine sandwich, which likewise remains to be described, as does the residence of the medieval kings of Hungary, the city of Székesfehérvár, now occupied by Ford and IBM, among others. Teabagging, once mentioned in Sex in the City, is considered nonconsensual in the context of hazing rituals. In Tebnine, east of Tyre, the inhabitants often dress fashionably and hang out in various cafes of an evening.

II

Other volumes may ignore, or so I imagine, the Abenaki, among whom there are no tribes recognized as such by the Bureau of Indian Affairs; perhaps the district of Atocha in Madrid is mentioned but not its railway station, which we are forever leaving. And what of the river Bzyb, in whose upper reaches grows the colorful bellflower Campanula mirabilis, whose profuse growth of one hundred flowers per plant has earned it the title of "Queen of Abkhazian flora?" Or of Denys Corbet, the "last poet" of Guernésiais? Likewise I'll wager you'd seek in vain for Tad Dameron, evening gowns, Gebirgsjäger, Louis Hjelmslev, or kalimbas. Not that I've looked. But imagined omissions are not necessarily imaginary ones. Muar, the hub of the Indonesian furniture industry, boasts four Pizza Huts, but in none of them can you purchase ptasie mleczko, a chocolate-covered meringue or milk soufflé candy whose Polish name signifies "unobtainable delicacy." Still, none of these can be found missing from an encyclopedia volume covering Spain through Technetium, and likewise only elsewhere would we feel the absence of ubiquinol, Watts, or the Supreme Court's decision in Yates v. United States, which J. Edgar Hoover declared "the greatest victory the Communist Party in America ever received," let alone any hint that the word "zydeco" might derive from the delicious phrase *Les haricots ne sont pas salé*s.

III

How the Vase Fell Off the Windowsill

In this enormous hospital
the given flower is still you
a most narrow passage
you found your way to the back
of the truth

I never got the chance to tell you
truth can be recombined
inside a shadow
the inverted diurnal world
where I should still admit
I am sorry

plush without testament
in a vase of water
my mistaken identity
never got the chance to tell you
your line drawings of air
help bear the heat of love

Wrong Number

Here's what passes for poetry
in one passerby's unreliable account

the sea flaps its nets
of futility

who's there, who's there

images pay no rent
but the echo carries

from what distance
could a cloud of dust
look that hard

The Smell of Burning Tires

Once before running out of breath
matching sky against sky

if your mind is not paranoid these days
you've got a big problem

scantily represented in the literature
of bridge and tunnel lyricism

not particularly frightened by my death
—the rest I think you know

a powdered eye
don't ask me about it now

in an atlas of cold weather
drawn to its inconclusion

Inverted Jenny

Your footsteps take me a long way
as on the radio I hear money singing
and wish I had more too
I'm feeling murky

my wheels grind increasingly slowly
to hear the sound of the distance
my love practices daily
an oracle on a stipend

an art for people who know nothing about it
if only you were in front of me
I wouldn't be able to look into your eyes

did anyone tell you this page might be haunted
the weather lasts so long
and the sky, overwhelming

Blinking Out

The moon is real
the moonlit ghost is real
but like a soft lens
unfit to be dreamed of
by philosophers of disappointment

many others know all this
and I write these lines to spite them
who knows who likes their sex with who
in place of the words you lost
the one you heard talking
it was never me

Seasonal Affective Disorder

Winter torn to bits
flickers down as propaganda
unrecovered thoughts
gathered in heaps around cars and bushes
but who cares

fog paints you into a gray Chinese landscape
even most whitened colors
grow leaden in the shadows

To Be Read in Silence

Hello forever
goodbye for now
figuring out the rules of the game
is the object of the game

overhead for personal items
whose name was never known
there's no place like no place
someone call the pleasure police because
mine's been stolen

Dead Drop

Let's do it wrong again
one last time
and turn out the light

some sublime etymologies
this one last fatigue
@sofuckedup.com
but pay no mind

recite
or try foldering
the last thing you remember

A Perfect Game

Each day seems to drop a line
could be my third or fourth debut
it's a title not a promise

oh sorry guys
you can make a copy
from memory

the phrase lingers in the air like an insane dancer
tell me what you want and I will bring it for you

to paint it would be pointless
without a saving drop of despair in the binder
(the film-forming part of the paint)

LES Air Shaft

Good curtains make good neighbors
wherever there's a pigeon on the loose
even with the monster of the week
everything turns out perfect in the end

full body, notes of dry fig and tobacco
the subtle caramel sweetness
of piled-up thoughts
seemingly shameless platonism exhibited here

but amiably peopled
and of fruit
in which mortality coils
waiting

waning
a young girl peeks at an old moon
and dreams of her all-nothingness

only love reminds you of love

And Nothing But

You can look in the mirror to practice crying
meanwhile words slip away
who could follow their braided repartee
each syllable a plan gone astray

last thought
best thought
next thought

do they realize they can see each other
the nights are getting longer
things it's too early to tell

that infernal andante
the answer is never "never"
straying down dead end words
how do I look in this whisky

Radio Free Love

For once the sounds moved toward us
we'd slipped them in

among memories hardly worth keeping
means-tested, addressing clouds

birds and the spirits of the dead
not to be discouraged

its feral form goes live before
your novelization of it gets written

that's how the lightning starts
when the weather gets strange

with thunder you can't hear
write it down now

before it takes off and our thoughts
self-interpenetrate

A Feeling of Blue
in memoriam, Matthew Wong

Is this a place
or just a future out of time
is it a branch fallen off the tree of sadness
to rejoin the famished earth
in harmless song
the one we call "Please get lots of love
to spread around evenly
as you go," that is, to scatter
as you wander deeper
into the forest where you find yourself lost
in love and no way out again

—but wherever you are
please call me when you get to the lobby
call me
when the waning sun gets its claws into
you
and the wind hacks off particles of skin
you hardly needed anyway
you can't close your eyes to what's already
dyed into your imagination
it stares at you from a spectral mirror
under your eyelid
which is always the one nearest
to the future clamor

of carrion birds or chemical bells
lodged in a temporal lobe
you feel like you've only
just started to hear it

IV
Last Poems

Living Within Your Meanings

It was early
the light was still hidden somewhere
a time of suffocation

but wait until the clock
ruins time completely
the bed a distorting mirror

we never heard the end of it
your new style of face
in sleep's tormented power

just remember
starlings do nothing in moderation

Gretchen's Law

I thought it was death pro-
nouncing my name
a plot to extinguish my silence but no

just bad moods driving out good
a specter haunting Brooklyn

yes, these are my own outages
collected workarounds
or an aliquot part

no, I didn't write them
just a minute of deep breathing to reduce stress
brought them briefly into view

and yet the torments of beauty
make me happiest
were we made this way on purpose

so diaphanous and disagreeable
how can you just forget
this shiver in which time contracts?

Sincerely, Your Target Language

Then there's that moment
life feels so soft
flesh cushioned by the flesh
of rose petals

you could let yourself fall into that
but through the matted down petals
a shiver of crunching stems
a scratching of thorns

little scarlet points of blood
multiply
with your tossing and turning
      skin breaks
with the branches

Floppy Disco

My blunt refusal to write today
my desire being desirable
my timing's been turned off

a night in which there's only one bright window
from which a lamp shouts its warning
it would have been no sort of enlightenment

some people remember
all that should have happened
but never did

take this rose, here's where you dance
think continually of those who are truly grating
those who believe they are universal
and those who do not

what a drag
to allow for the dissolution of time
with our luxury worries
like what's the latest superfood

My Bad

I

The crickets said it was over
we'd set the earth to rest
between one breath and the next
a world dreams itself dry

II

No cure for the marvelous
but lacking staff to stuff so many radioactive animal parts
into the mouth of a furnace
the citizens rallied by candlelight

is there anything about which nothing has been said
a country where once I meant to found a ruin
or attend a school for gilding icons

speaking truth to pathos
she solved some small pinkish riddles
the only reason that I think I think

III

The crickets call it a night
our planet deep in its slumbers

where desiccation was just a forlorn hope
love goes in one ear and out the other

will wonders never cease
they never give the breakdown you deserve
throwing stray objects out the window is no fun
when light and terrible heat collect in your ballet shoes without
     instruction

the dictionary's lengthy entry in secret
to build up your breath
where no one's raised the funding for a memory farm

eating silence all day long
at least until a secret spreads its wings
her space folds itself around you

IV

If only I glimpse it for a moment
your secret safest in me

figure ground down to scratches
of those I most regret missing

and never knew how you disliked them
etc. ad libitum

The Shape of Jazz to Come

Your eyes were lit for the sake of this window
through which things
you thought were invisible
can be still less visible but heard

neighbors keep themselves to themselves
and day by day become less familiar with their street
where flapping wildly under asthmatic clouds
some death draws a solitary bird into its vortex

your eyes the color of seraphim
drawn or drowned in plum-colored ink
found two willing targets
soon blurred by rain

and that same death
though prudence forbid that we say it
marks us down on a long to-do list
we know him only by name

but wait! wait! that thin asthmatic sky
breathes its last tuneless music
into your open mouth
and shadows your half-closed eyes, but why?

Selective Memory

in memoriam, Steve Dalachinsky

Space, such a fragile invention
to write it is like wrapping a tourniquet
but when all those sparrows engage in their filibuster
there's nothing you can do but listen
their flowery haiku explain
what's on the other side of death
is death: simple

With any consonant as their horizon
the vowels form a single very fine substance
that pervades the entire universe

The only halo is a half note
and in a poem you once transcribed
each word rhymes with a truth
one person at a time can hear

Some birds or musicians may pause for a moment of silence
recalling your rapt attention
an eye narrowed down on the feathered vibration of a trackless
      foreafter[1]
which might have meant only you could hear it
amidst the twittering that they use
to mask an ultrasonic conversation
it reminds you of a rain-soaked voice
you once started to think you'd be in love with

The rain falls only in your profligate heart
the dew gathers on your petals of enjoyment
the clouds that float wispily in someone's sun-filled voice
slip quietly into the sea
like ink absorbed
into the pores of your fingers

---

1   This word, as far as I know, is Steve's invention—found in "For Charles-Henri Ford—Another I Did Not Know," Brooklyn Rail, April–May 2003.

Licking River

I lick the pollen from the nooks and crannies of your voice
it had settled there in anticipation

the wind shifts direction like a verse
you once impressed on my lips

before I touched them to the mirror
and looked to find your secret name there
a woman who broke her eyes by crying

niche empath cutie
and all the stars barricaded inside your skull

looking with the third eye
all signs point to yes

nothing matters more to me than this
come to me, come into my army

Broken Wing Display

in memoriam, Sean Bonney

The sun on its way out of there
horizon forced to give up its secret
the last word on the majesty of the sexes

   —and your most recent bird
the black seed from which a whole sky is born
whose words are our most remote ancestors
their syllables collapse into heaps of silence

a dozen pockets where you never find your keys
echoes multiply in the locked box where you store them
like a heart filled with laughter
your broken teeth tore to pieces

Emergency Landing on Water

Autumn memory defers
a word neither yes nor no
found scratched in the margin of a discarded notebook
a passing visitor
left in suspense upon a table

it was an absorbed neighborhood
you touched up into the past
what with all the rain and fog you ever imagined
wrapped around your fluttering self

escape lights will show you
the way to the exits
stars looking all serious and old-fashioned
are just ideas you blurted out

or compiled into a sheaf
of unplugged luminosity
found only by taking a wrong turn
your beauty becomes metaphorical

Theremin

Can a feeling be a mistake
later run out of exceptions
you see who we are
before we even know it

you asked me what comes next
after love
well it's not over yet
energy exchanged as heat or work

we did away with all of our cases
but the body still has its pleats
the only unit of meaning is the world
a vibrating thing

it all still felt like fiction
in the hours or years since we last met

In a Previous Life
for Douglas Crase and Frank Polach

I used to hide out in a cinder block garage
set apart in an indecisive landscape
waiting under barren skies in which
even a child's kite wears a look

of partial bereavement
practically nameless, a tangible sign
that lingers longingly in its own aftermath
its loneliness granted permission

are there still radios in this world
among the piles of sad merchandise
if you know how to broadcast a truth

let's see whether I know how to hear it
if something else
hang on to it until I've left the room

Notes Toward a Code of Best Practice

Glancing toward the sources of wisdom
I could just glimpse the back of my mind
drifting off into the distance
maybe catch it on its way back around

it was only then
your past lost its predictability
darkness opened onto a wet body
I'm taking in later for repairs

the skin of a human being like that of a ripe fruit
when pierced
leaks saturated sweetness

whose presence cohabits with D—th
and feeds you enough words to talk with
to update our situation with reckless accuracy

Memories Have Such Delicate Skin

Her voice was soft and pink
swallowed the whole of a pockmarked landscape
in which every single thing was possibility
her aria, a partial eclipse of the moon

recitative a forest, a house for animals
and people who've resigned
from human community
leaving more room

for we the postponed living
to frame pointed statements of intent
we hold together in the shape of doubt

but then the space left behind
less elusive than the one she'd occupied
how these whistling creatures nest in the shadows of cities

Code Vein Magic

The room tone not quite innocent
outside, abundant cloud cover
one player requests the subject be made more perspicuous
unaware this would also make it evanesce

none the worse for where it's been
or even not been
taking exception to syntax
the successor to the rib cage

with one last liter of residual air
I was real before it was fashionable
a face in the crowd, the life of a party
whose half-life as commander of shadows

and kingpin of contrails suggests
if beauty is as beauty does
you'd break open a dictionary just to watch
the words pour out

Soft Opening

Night is a curtain you draw
across the frosted glass of my eyes
shadows thrown on this pane are not a movie
or poetry mined from its own absence

emotional agriculture: you wait for my eyes
to ripen

I can't get excited about nihilism
start wearing skin inside out
who knows why
but I dreamed you came back yelling
how come you never wrote me that elegy, you bastard
later find it lying among scattered papers

some examples of extended technique
flutter tonguing, circular breathing
I chew the warmth of your open palm
whose taste is like the light glancing off

Acknowledgments

Many of these poems, which were composed between 2014 and 2019, have previously appeared in these print and online magazines: *Bennington Review, Black Sun Lit*, the *Brooklyn Rail, Caesura, Can We Have Our Ball Back, Dispatches from the Poetry Wars, Dusie, Fragen, Galatea Resurrects, GUEST, Harper's Magazine, Hyperallergic Weekend, Live!, Marsh Hawk Review, NOON: Journal of the Short Poem*, the *Quarterless Review*, and *Snow*. Others were first published these books and exhibition catalogues: *Blood Flames Revisited*, ed. by Phong Bui (New York: Paul Kasmin Gallery, 2014); *Mel Chin: The Funk & Wag From A to Z* (Houston: The Menil Collection, 2014); *Noon on the Moon: Poetics Series #4*, ed. by Fiona Bryson and Keren Cytter (Berlin: Sternberg Press, 2015). Heartfelt thanks to all the editors and publishers who so kindly made space for my writing.

Several of the poems were written thanks to a residency at the Isabella Stewart Gardner Museum, Boston, and performed with music by Marianne Nowottny at the museum's Calderwood Hall on April 2, 2015, and then at Bas Fisher Invitational, Miami, April 7, 2015. Special thanks to Pieranna Cavalchini of the Isabella Stewart Gardner Museum and Naomi Fisher of Bas Fisher Invitational.

All of the words in the poems, along with so many others that accompany and give them their setting, have been used by millions of others before me, known and unknown, and will be used by millions after. My highest gratitude is to them.

About the Author

Barry Schwabsky was born in Paterson, New Jersey, and lives in Long Island, New York. He is art critic for *The Nation* as well as co-editor of international reviews for *Artforum* and has written many books of criticism and poetry. Among these are *Book Left Open in the Rain, Trembling Hand Equilibrium,* and *Heretics of Language,* all published by Black Square Editions.

Black Square Editions was started in 1999 with the intention of publishing translations of little-known books by well-known poets and fiction writers, as well as the work of emerging and established authors. After twenty-three years, we are still proceeding book by book.

Black Square Editions—a subsidiary of Off the Park Press, Inc, a tax-exempt (501c3) nonprofit organization—would like to thank the following for their support.

Tim Barry
Robert Bunker
Catherine Kehoe
Taylor Moore
Goldman Sachs
Pittsburgh Foundation Grant
Miles McEnery Gallery (New York, New York)
I.M. of Emily Mason & Wolf Kahn
Galerie Lelong & Co. (Paris, France)
Bernard Jacobson Gallery (London, England)
Saturnalia Books
& Anonymous Donors

Black Square Editions

Richard Anders *The Footprints of One Who Has Not Stepped Forth* (trans. Andrew Joron)

Andrea Applebee *Aletheia*

Eve Aschheim and Chris Daubert *Episodes with Wayne Thiebaud: Interviews*

Eve Aschheim *Eve Aschheim: Recent Work*

Anselm Berrigan *Pregrets*

Garrett Caples *The Garrett Caples Reader*

Marcel Cohen *Walls (Anamneses)* (trans. Brian Evenson and Joanna Howard)

Lynn Crawford *Fortification Resort*

Lynn Crawford *Simply Separate People, Two*

Thomas Devaney *You Are the Battery*

Ming Di (Editor) *New Poetry from China: 1917–2017* (trans. various)

Joseph Donahue *Red Flash on a Black Field*

Rachel Blau DuPlessis *Late Work*

Marcella Durand *To husband is to tender*

Rosalyn Drexler *To Smithereens*

Brian Evenson *Dark Property*

Serge Fauchereau *Complete Fiction* (trans. John Ashbery and Ron Padgett)

Jean Frémon *Painting* (trans. Brian Evenson)

Jean Frémon *The Paradoxes of Robert Ryman* (trans. Brian Evenson)

Ludwig Hohl *Ascent* (trans. Donna Stonecipher)

Isabelle Baladine Howald *phantomb* (trans. Eléna Rivera)

Philippe Jaccottet *Ponge, Pastures, Prairies* (trans. John Taylor)

Ann Jäderlund *Which once had been meadow* (trans. Johannes Göransson)

Franck André Jamme *Extracts from the Life of a Beetle* (trans. Michael Tweed)

Franck André Jamme *Another Silent Attack* (trans. Michael Tweed)

Franck André Jamme *The Recitation of Forgetting* (trans. John Ashbery)

Andrew Joron *Fathom*

Karl Larsson *FORM/FORCE* (trans. Jennifer Hayashida)

Hervé Le Tellier *Atlas Inutilis* (trans. Cole Swensen)

Eugene Lim *The Strangers*

Michael Leong *Cutting Time with a Knife*

Michael Leong *Words on Edge*

Gary Lutz *I Looked Alive*

Michèle Métail *Earth's Horizons: Panorama* (trans. Marcella Durand)

Michèle Métail *Identikits* (trans. Philip Terry)

Albert Mobilio *Me with Animal Towering*

Albert Mobilio *Touch Wood*

Albert Mobilio *Games & Stunts*

Albert Mobilio *Same Faces*

Pascalle Monnier *Bayart* (trans. Cole Swensen)

Christopher Nealon *The Joyous Age*

María Negroni *Berlin Interlude* (trans. Michelle Gil-Montero)

Doug Nufer *Never Again*

John Olson *Echo Regime*

John Olson *Free Stream Velocity*

Eva Kristina Olsson *The Angelgreen Sacrament* (trans. Johannes Göransson)

Juan Sánchez Peláez *Air on the Air: Selected Poems* (trans. Guillermo Parra)

Véronique Pittolo *Hero* (trans. Laura Mullen)

Pierre Reverdy *Prose Poems* (trans. Ron Padgett)

Pierre Reverdy *Haunted House* (trans. John Ashbery)

Pierre Reverdy *The Song of the Dead* (trans. Dan Bellm)

Pierre Reverdy *Georges Braque: A Methodical Adventure* (trans. Andrew Joron
and Rose Vekony)

Valérie-Catherine Richez *THIS NOWHERE WHERE*

Barry Schwabsky *Book Left Open in the Rain*

Barry Schwabsky *Trembling Hand Equilibrium*

Barry Schwabsky *Heretics of Language*

Jeremy Sigler *Crackpot*

Jørn H. Sværen *Queen of England* (trans. Jørn H. Sværen)

Genya Turovskaya *The Breathing Body of This Thought*

Matvei Yankelevich *Some Worlds for Dr. Vogt*